SNAKES SET I

PYTHONS

Megan M. Gunderson
ABDO Publishing Company

Published by ABDO Publishing Company, 8000 West 78th Street, Edina, Minnesota 55439. Copyright © 2011 by Abdo Consulting Group, Inc. International copyrights reserved in all countries. No part of this book may be reproduced in any form without written permission from the publisher. The Checkerboard Library™ is a trademark and logo of ABDO Publishing Company.

Printed in the United States of America, North Mankato, Minnesota.
042010
092010

 PRINTED ON RECYCLED PAPER

Cover Photo: Getty Images
Interior Photos: Corbis p. 20; Getty Images p. 17; iStockphoto p. 15;
    National Geographic Stock pp. 7, 11; Peter Arnold pp. 5, 18; Photo Researchers p. 9;
    Photolibrary p. 21

Editor: BreAnn Rumsch
Art Direction & Cover Design: Neil Klinepier

Library of Congress Cataloging-in-Publication Data

Gunderson, Megan M., 1981-
 Pythons / Megan M. Gunderson.
    p. cm. -- (Snakes)
 Includes index.
 ISBN 978-1-61613-437-2
 1. Pythons--Juvenile literature. I. Title.
 QL666.O67G86 2011
 597.96'78--dc22
                      2010013421

CONTENTS

PYTHONS

Some of the longest snakes on Earth are pythons. Like all snakes, scales and stretchy skin cover these vertebrates. And, pythons slither through their **habitats** without the help of limbs.

Pythons are cold-blooded. This simply means they rely on heat from their surroundings to warm up. To avoid getting too hot, they cool down in shade or shelter.

Pythons belong to the family **Pythonidae**. There are at least 28 species of pythons in this family. They are similar to boa constrictors and anacondas. Like those snakes, pythons often kill their prey by constriction. They coil around unlucky creatures and squeeze them to death!

Pythons must control their body temperature to survive.

SIZES

Many python species are huge. In fact, the reticulated python is the longest snake in the world. It can reach 33 feet (10 m) in length and weigh up to 250 pounds (113 kg)! The African rock python can also grow more than 30 feet (9 m) long.

Not all pythons break records, but several other species are plenty long! For example, the amethystine python reaches 28 feet (8.5 m) in length. The Indian python can grow up to 23 feet (7 m) long.

The world's smallest python is the pygmy python. It is also known as the anthill python. This snake grows less than 2 feet (.6 m) long. The Children's python is nearly as small. It reaches just over 3 feet (1 m) in length.

An amethystine python

COLORS

The many different python species come in a wide variety of colors. Some pythons are among the most beautifully colored snakes in the world. For example, adult green tree pythons are brilliant green.

A python's name can be a clue to its coloring. The white-lipped python has white scales bordering its mouth. The blood python has a wide range of colors. But some are red or orange, as their name suggests.

Special patterns help pythons blend into their **habitats**. The reticulated python's name comes from the way it looks. It has a reticulated, or netlike, pattern down its back. A large, blotchy pattern covers the Indian python.

Young green tree pythons can be bright yellow or even red!

WHERE THEY LIVE

Pythons don't just have a variety of looks. They also live in many different **habitats**. Some pythons live mostly in trees. Yet most spend their time on the ground. These land-loving snakes often live near water. They are excellent swimmers.

A python's name may hint at where it lives. The green tree python hangs over branches high up in rain forests. The brown water python prefers living in swamps and creeks.

The Bismarck ringed python is named for the Bismarck **Archipelago** in the Pacific Ocean. It lives

Australia's rain forests are home to many pythons.

in rain forests and near plantations. It may also
spend time in burrows. The African rock python
enjoys rocky areas as well as woodlands and
savannas. It also lives in swamps and rain forests.

WHERE THEY ARE FOUND

Members of the family **Pythonidae** live in Africa, Asia, and Australia, and on many Pacific islands. African rock pythons are the largest snakes in Africa. Their range covers central and eastern Africa.

Green tree pythons live in northern Australia and on the island of New Guinea. Carpet pythons live in northern, eastern, and southern Australia. They live in southern New Guinea, too.

Reticulated pythons and Indian pythons are the largest snake species in Asia. Both species live in Southeast Asia. The reticulated python lives in India as well. It is also common in the Philippines, New Guinea, and other Pacific islands.

Where Pythons Live

Detail Area

ASIA

AFRICA

Pacific
Ocean

Indian
Ocean

Atlantic
Ocean

AUSTRALIA

N

SENSES

Pythons are excellent predators because they have keen senses. For example, they have a good sense of sight. Snakes are especially good at spotting movement.

A snake can hear, but it doesn't listen through **external** ears. Instead, its lower jaw detects vibrations in the ground. These vibrations might be from a predator approaching or from prey wandering by. They travel through the snake's jawbones to its inner ears.

Unlike many animals, a snake doesn't smell only through its nostrils. It also smells using its long, forked tongue. Flicking out the tongue picks up scent particles in the air. The tongue brings the odors to the Jacobson's **organ** in the mouth. This organ analyzes the scents.

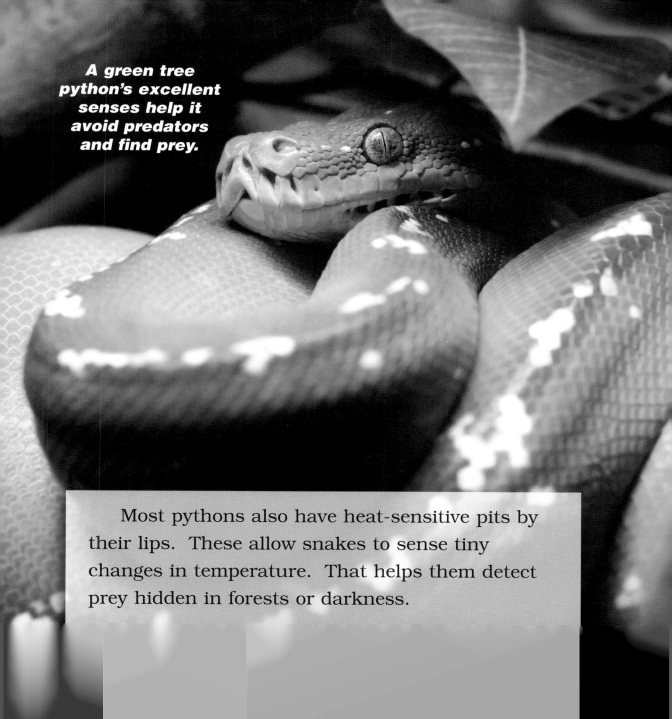

A green tree python's excellent senses help it avoid predators and find prey.

Most pythons also have heat-sensitive pits by their lips. These allow snakes to sense tiny changes in temperature. That helps them detect prey hidden in forests or darkness.

DEFENSE

Many pythons seem like giants, but they still have enemies! Eagles, lions, and leopards will go after adult pythons. In addition, smaller pythons must watch out for large insects and even other snakes. Humans threaten pythons, too. They cause **habitat** destruction and kill pythons for their skins.

Pythons defend themselves in a variety of ways. They often rely on camouflage to stay hidden. If found, pythons may first try to escape.

When that doesn't work, a python tries another defense. The reticulated python hisses loudly and opens its mouth wide. It also puffs up its body to appear bigger. These actions make it look threatening!

The ball python tries a different method. It coils up into a ball! This protects the snake's head from attack.

As a last resort, pythons will strike out and bite an enemy. They do not release **venom**. But, their mouths are lined with rows of sharp teeth!

A blood python can stay hidden in leaf litter for days at a time.

FOOD

A hungry python's diet depends on its size. These snakes eat lizards and birds as well as **rodents** and other mammals. A large meal might take days to **digest**.

A python's jawbones move apart so it can swallow large meals.

The Children's python eats geckos, frogs, bats, and snakes. The black-headed python also enjoys snakes, including **venomous** species. The carpet python and several others help control rat populations.

African rock pythons feast on goats and antelopes. These huge pythons and reticulated pythons have even been known to eat humans.

A python hides and waits for prey to wander by. Its camouflage keeps it out of sight until the prey comes very close. Then, the snake strikes out!

The python grabs the unlucky creature in its mouth. Then, it usually wraps itself around the animal. The snake squeezes until the prey can no longer breathe. Finally, it swallows its meal whole.

BABIES

Baby pythons hatch from eggs. The number of eggs a female lays varies greatly. The ball python lays just 4 to 8 eggs at a time. The huge reticulated python lays as many as 100!

Children's python mothers coil around their eggs.

Most female pythons coil around their eggs until they hatch. Some pythons also **incubate** their eggs. They twitch their muscles to create heat, which helps the eggs hatch faster. For snakes, this is an unusual habit.

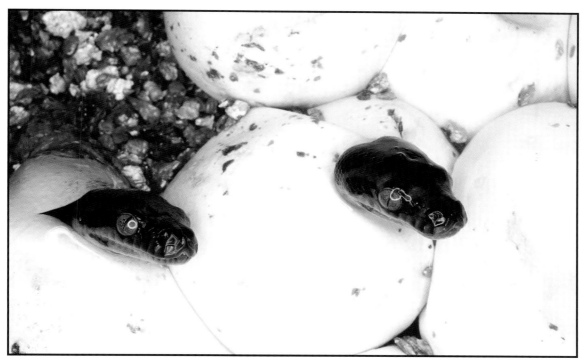

A baby snake has a temporary egg tooth on the end of its snout. It uses this sharp tool to slash open its egg.

Once pythons hatch from their eggs, they must survive on their own. Soon after birth, they **shed** for the first time. They continue to do this every time they outgrow their skin. As adults, they will also shed whenever their skin becomes injured or worn. Pythons survive up to 35 years.

GLOSSARY

archipelago (ahr-kuh-PEH-luh-goh) - a group of islands.

digest - to break down food into simpler substances the body can absorb.

external - of, relating to, or being on the outside.

habitat - a place where a living thing is naturally found.

incubate - to keep eggs warm so they will hatch.

organ - a part of an animal or a plant composed of several kinds of tissues. An organ performs a specific function. The heart, liver, gallbladder, and intestines are organs of an animal.

Pythonidae (peye-THAHN-uh-dee) - the scientific name for the python family. This family includes at least 28 snake species that live in Africa, Asia, and Australia.

rodent - any of several related animals that have large front teeth for gnawing. Common rodents include mice, squirrels, and beavers.

savanna - a grassy plain with few or no trees.

shed - to cast off hair, feathers, skin, or other coverings or parts by a natural process.

venom - a poison produced by some animals and insects. It usually enters a victim through a bite or a sting. Something that produces venom is venomous.

WEB SITES

To learn more about pythons, visit ABDO Publishing Company on the World Wide Web at **www.abdopublishing.com**. Web sites about pythons are featured on our Book Links page. These links are routinely monitored and updated to provide the most current information available.

INDEX

A

Africa 12
Asia 12
Australia 12

B

babies 20, 21
body 8, 16, 20

C

camouflage 8, 16, 19
cold-blooded 4
color 8
constriction 4, 19

D

defense 8, 16, 17

E

ears 14
eggs 20, 21

F

food 4, 14, 15, 18, 19

H

habitat 4, 8, 10, 11, 12, 16
head 16
heat-sensitive pits 15

J

Jacobson's organ 14
jaws 14

L

life span 21

M

mouth 8, 14, 15, 16, 17, 19

N

nostrils 14

P

Pythonidae (family) 4, 12

S

scales 4, 8
senses 14, 15
shedding 21
size 4, 6, 12, 16, 18, 19, 20
skin 4, 16, 21

T

teeth 17
threats 14, 16, 17
tongue 14

V

vertebrates 4
vibrations 14